The Good Life Weight Loss Surgery Cookbook:

Recipes for Eating Healthfully and Happily After Your Bariatric Surgery

The Good Life Weight Loss Surgery Cookbook:

Recipes for Eating Healthfully and Happily After Your Bariatric Surgery

By Rosemary Dolloff

Copyright 2015 Rosemary Dolloff. All Rights Reserved

Disclaimer: *This book contains general information regarding diet and nutrition that is based on author's own knowledge and experiences. It is published for general reference and is not intended to be a substitute for the advice of your doctor, dietitian, nutritionist, or other health care provider. The publisher and the author disclaim any personal liability, either directly or indirectly, for the information contained within and encourage you to discuss with your doctor any questions or concerns you may have. Although the author and the publisher have made every effort to ensure the accuracy and completeness of the information contained within, we assume no responsibility for errors, inaccuracies, omissions and inconsistencies.*

Dedication:
To Nate, Chandra and Jackson
For their patience and love

Table of Contents

Introduction: What I've Learned 1

Instructions 3

Breakfast 5

    Breakfast Smoothie 6
    Breakfast Custard 8
    Omelet 9
    Frittata with Pasta 11
    Ham and Cheese Crustless Quiche 13

Lunch 15
    Asparagus Salad 16

Shrimp and Avocado Salad 17

Potato and Red Pepper Salad 18

Tomato Salad with Fresh Mozzarella 19

Chicken and Apple Slaw 20

Dinner 21

Shrimp and Asparagus Stir-Fry................... 22

Baked Salmon with Pesto 24

Italian Sole 25

Baked Orange Sole 27

Pan-Fried Scallops and Summer Squash 28

Pan-Roasted Chicken 29

Chicken and Pesto..................................... 31

Grilled Chicken Italian Style....................... 32

Chicken Lettuce Wraps.............................. 34

Chicken Tortellini Salad 35

Turkey Chili 37

Stir-Fried Turkey and Broccoli................... 38

Ham and Winter Squash Soup..................... 40

Grilled Pork Chop with Chutney Sauce 41

Pork Kebabs... 43

Pan-Fried Sirloin with Mushroom Gravy 44

Meatloaf 46

Beef Stew 47

Lamb Burgers with Feta Cheese 49

Stuffed Portobello Mushrooms 50

Green Beans with Bacon 52

Baked Tofu 53

Snacks 55

Protein Powder Shake 56

Protein Bars 58

Ready-to-Drink Protein Shakes 60

Fat-Free Low-Sugar Yogurt 61

Cheese Stick and Fruit 62

Introduction: What I've Learned

When I had my weight loss surgery two years ago, I was both excited and scared. I was excited because I knew I had made the right choice in having the surgery (I had a sleeve gastrectomy), and I trusted my medical team 100 percent. I was scared because I knew it would bring big changes to my life and some of them wouldn't be easy.

The hardest thing for me about the surgery process was cooking. I was emotionally prepared for giving up things like soda, and adapting to the small food portions. But I had enjoyed food before my surgery and considered myself a good cook. When the dietitian presented me with the diet plan during my pre-operative counseling, my heart sank. I thought, how am I ever going to cook like this? Another thing to consider was my family. With an average-weight husband and two healthy teenagers at home, I dreaded the thought of cooking one meal for them and a separate one for me.

But I wanted the weight loss and health benefits strongly enough that I decided to go forward with the surgery. I had some frank, productive talks with my husband and kids. I explained that high protein, low fat food would be at the center of our table from now on, and the fatty, unhealthy foods that had brought me to this point would be off limits for me, and an occasional indulgence for them. To my everlasting gratitude, they were completely on board with this, because they wanted me to reach my goals.

What remained, then, was applying my skill as a cook to the new task of preparing a wide variety of healthy, nourishing, satisfying meals that I could serve to my family while modifying them for my diet plan after surgery. And they had to be easy to fix – no long lists of ingredients or exotic food items found only in big city specialty markets. I quickly learned that planning is the key, and I applied myself to my new task with gusto, starting a few months before I went in for my surgery.

The results of what I've learned are contained in this book.

To your health and happiness,
– *Rosemary Dolloff*

Instructions

My instructions are to follow your doctor's instructions. Period. Don't cheat on your eating plan if you want to lose weight. Keep your portions small and watch the total grams of fat, as recommended by your medical team.

Most of my recipes taste fine pureed while you're still in the soft food stage, but blender food isn't for everyone. I coped with the soft food weeks by eating a lot of breakfast smoothies and custard (the first two recipes in the Breakfast section). There's such a nice selection of flavorings you can add, and they're so smooth and appetizing that I never got tired of them. For pureeing foods, I found that a food processor was a must-have item.

All of the recipes are tasty enough to share with family – simply multiply the ingredients. If you're several weeks out of surgery, note that most of them are one cup per serving, which fits perfectly with my eating plan. In my early weeks after surgery when my portions were still tiny, my family enjoyed the extra portions I couldn't eat yet.

Most bariatric clinics advise introducing new foods slowly, one food at a time. Although your doctor might have given you the green light to eat nearly anything you used to eat, that doesn't mean your stomach will cooperate. I learned to be cautious and go slowly as I tried new recipes.

The nutritional information for each recipe is from the USDA's nutrition data and the labeling on packaged ingredients. It's approximate because items like eggs, fruits, and vegetables don't come in standard sizes, and everybody chops and dices their portions a bit differently. But it's close enough for you to make a pretty good estimate.

Enjoy the process as you make your journey to an attractive, healthy new you!

Breakfast

I quickly learned that the first meal of my day is the most important. I've gone without food since the evening of the day before, and my reserves are starting to get low. Breakfast keeps my mind alert and my energy level high throughout the morning, even if it's just a simple fruit smoothie with protein powder. As always, planning is the key. Prepare your ingredients in the evening before you go to bed and set your utensils out on the kitchen counter so you can make breakfast happen in a jiffy.

Breakfast Smoothie

I like using plain yogurt and adding artificial sweetener to taste, instead of the flavored yogurts which are very high in sugar. Whey protein powder is a better choice than soy protein, which I find hard to digest. You'll be eating a lot of these, because they're so delicious and convenient, so you might want to buy a specialized smoothie blender that includes a couple of serving-size cups with to-go lids.

Basic smoothie:

- 1/2 cup nonfat plain yogurt
- 1/4 cup skim milk
- 1/4 cup water
- 1 scoop whey protein powder: choose a low-sugar or sugar-free brand like Designer Whey or Met-RX
- 1 packet sugar-free sweetener

Flavorings:

- 1/2 cup diced fresh fruit, any variety (choose ONE OR MORE totaling 1/2 cup)

- Strawberries
- Raspberries
- Peaches
- Apricots
- Oranges
- Kiwi fruit
- OR – 1 teaspoon sugar-free flavor syrup such as Torani
- OR – 1 teaspoon cocoa powder

Mix all ingredients in blender until smooth. Drink immediately.

- ✓ Yield: 1 cup
- ✓ Calories: 213
- ✓ Protein: 32 grams
- ✓ Carbohydrate: 16.2 grams
- ✓ Fat: 2.4 grams

ROSEMARY DOLLOFF

Breakfast Custard

A mix of eggs and egg whites keeps the fat down while giving this custard the same appealing, creamy texture as its full-fat cousin. Pick up a set of four custard cups for easy baking and an appealing presentation at the breakfast table. This recipe is ideal for the soft food stage after your surgery.

- 2 cups skim milk
- 2 whole eggs
- 1/2 cup egg substitute
- 2 Tablespoons granulated non-sugar sweetener

Preheat oven to 325. Boil 6 cups of water on the stove top or microwave it to boiling point. Scald the 2 cups of milk in a medium size saucepan and cool until warm to the touch. Whisk the eggs and egg substitute together gently in a large bowl. Mix in sweetener. Slowly whisk the milk into the bowl with the eggs. Pour into 4 ovenproof custard baking dishes and place them in a shallow pan on oven rack. Pour the hot water around the cups about 1 inch deep. Bake for 40 to 45 minutes. Serve warm or chilled.

- ✓ Yield: four 1-cup servings
- ✓ Calories: 125
- ✓ Protein: 15 grams
- ✓ Carbohydrate: 8 grams
- ✓ Fat: 3 grams

Omelet

Omelets are high in protein, plus you can take advantage of last night's steamed vegetable from the fridge. My cooking technique is simple, with easy cleanup afterward, and produces a light, tender result.

Basic omelet:
- 1 large egg
- 2 Tablespoons egg substitute
- 2 Tablespoons skim milk
- Cooking spray

Fillings: (choose any two)

- 1/4 cup chopped sweet onion
- 1/4 cup chopped green or red bell pepper
- 1/2 cup chopped steamed vegetable left over from dinner (broccoli, green beans, cauliflower, etc.)

Spray an 8 inch nonstick frying pan with cooking spray. Saute filling ingredients over medium heat, tossing occasionally with a spatula. Beat the egg, egg substitute, and milk in a medium size bowl with a whisk until foamy. Distribute the filling ingredients evenly across one half of the frying pan. Pour in the eggs and tilt the pan so they spread evenly across the bottom and surround the filling ingredients. Reduce heat to low and cover with a tight-fitting lid. Check the eggs every two minutes until the surface is firm. Fold omelet in half and serve immediately.

- ✓ Yield: 1 cup
- ✓ Calories: 152
- ✓ Protein: 12.7 grams
- ✓ Carbohydrate: 11.4 grams
- ✓ Fat: 6.4 grams

Frittata with Pasta

A frittata is similar to an omelet but is served flat, like a pizza. Italian flavorings are popular with this dish. If you have an ovenproof frying pan, you can sear the cheese topping under the broiler before serving to make it puff up almost double in size, like a cake. Be careful – the handle will be hot!

- 1/2 cup hollow cooked pasta left over from dinner (macaroni, shells, or manicotti)
- 1/2 cup cubed zucchini or yellow summer squash
- 1/2 cup sliced fresh mushrooms
- Cooking spray
- 1 large egg
- 2 Tablespoons egg substitute
- 2 Tablespoons skim milk
- 1/4 cup shredded low-fat mozzarella cheese

Spray an 8 inch nonstick frying pan with cooking spray. Toss the pasta, zucchini, and mushrooms over medium-high heat until softened. Beat the egg, egg substitute, and milk in a medium size bowl with a whisk until foamy. Pour in the eggs and tilt the pan so they fill the pasta. Reduce heat to low and cover with a tight-fitting lid. Check the eggs every two minutes until the surface is firm. Remove from heat, top with cheese, and cover until cheese is melted.

- ✓ Yield: 1-1/2 cup
- ✓ Calories: 257
- ✓ Protein: 22 grams
- ✓ Carbohydrate: 18 grams
- ✓ Fat: 10.8 grams

Ham and Cheese Crustless Quiche

This dish needs to be baked, so it won't work so well on weekdays, but it's a nice treat if you want something special on the weekend. Without a crust, the fat and calories stay reasonably low. If you're only feeding yourself, cut the quiche into six wedges, store one or two in the fridge, and freeze the rest in their own tightly sealed bags.

- 2 eggs
- 1/2 cup egg substitute
- 1 cup low-fat ricotta cheese
- 1 cup fat-free sour cream
- 1 cup low-fat shredded Monterey jack cheese
- 1/4 cup grated Parmesan cheese
- 2 Tablespoons chopped sweet onion
- 1 cup fresh sliced mushrooms
- 2 cups diced ham
- Cooking spray

Preheat oven to 350. Spray an 8 x 8 inch square pan or 9 inch round deep dish pie pan with cooking spray. Whisk the eggs, egg substitute, sour cream, jack cheese, ricotta, and parmesan in a large mixing bowl. Spread the ham, mushrooms and onions evenly over the bottom of the baking pan. Pour the liquid ingredients over it. Bake 30-45 minutes until firm. Test by inserting the tip of a table knife in the center to see if it comes out clean.

- ✓ Yield: Six 1/2-cup servings
- ✓ Calories: 273
- ✓ Protein: 25 grams
- ✓ Carbohydrate: 9 grams
- ✓ Fat: 14 grams

Lunch

I work as office manager in a busy setting, so I usually eat lunch on the fly on weekdays. Packing a homemade lunch in a lunch tote with an ice pack makes it easy to say, "thanks but no thanks," when the rest of the office orders takeout. I have a nice collection of leakproof containers, and I make liberal use of zip-close plastic bags to keep perishable ingredients separate from each other until I'm ready to eat them. A stash of paper plates, plastic cutlery, and disposable bowls in my overhead storage bin makes lunch at work almost like eating at home!

Asparagus Salad

Asparagus makes a fine salad. Chilled and topped off with a tart dressing, it's delectable, and the hard-cooked egg provides the protein. This salad can be taken to work if kept chilled.

6 asparagus spears, baked or boiled
1 Tablespoon diced red onion
2 Tablespoons chopped red bell pepper
1 chopped hard-boiled egg

Mix well. Just before eating, dress with:
2 Tablespoons light salad dressing (red wine vinaigrette, Asian sesame, or honey mustard)

Yield: 1 cup
Calories: 151
Protein: 8.7 grams
Carbohydrate: 8.4 grams
Fat: 9.6 grams

Shrimp and Avocado Salad

This satisfying salad is worthy of any real deli. Spritz the avocado with lemon juice if you don't plan to eat it right away to keep it green.

- 1 cup baby leaf lettuce
- 1/2 avocado peeled and cut into chunks
- 1/2 medium size tomato, cut into wedges
- 1/4 cup canned shrimp, drained

Mix well. Just before eating, dress with:
1 Tablespoon light ranch or light caesar dressing

- ✓ Yield: 1 cup
- ✓ Calories: 216
- ✓ Protein: 9.6 grams
- ✓ Carbohydrate: 14 grams
- ✓ Fat: 14.7 grams

ROSEMARY DOLLOFF

Potato and Red Pepper Salad

This is a variation on my grandmother's German potato salad recipe. Potatoes run high in carbohydrate, so compensate by keeping them low for your other two meals today. The walnuts are there for protein, and because they taste great!

- 1 cup cooked potatoes, cubed (use last night's leftovers)
- 1 Tablespoon chopped red bell pepper
- 1 Tablespoon chopped green onion tops
- 2 Tablespoons chopped walnuts

Mix well. Just before eating, dress with:
1 Tablespoon light Russian, caesar, or honey mustard dressing

- ✓ Yield: 1.5 cup
- ✓ Calories: 263
- ✓ Protein: 5.3 grams
- ✓ Carbohydrate: 35.4 grams
- ✓ Fat: 12.4 grams

Tomato Salad with Fresh Mozzarella

Fresh mozzarella cheese is white in color and is more moist than its aged counterpart. It has a lovely mild flavor and pairs blissfully with tomatoes and other fresh vegetables. Look for it in the specialty cheese section of the deli at your grocery store. If you can't find it, a brick of regular mozzarella tastes great in this salad too.

- 1 medium size ripe tomato, cut into wedges
- 2 ounces fresh or aged mozzarella cheese
- 1 Tablespoon chopped green bell pepper
- 1 Tablespoon chopped sweet white onion
- 1 teaspoon dried basil or 2 Tablespoons fresh basil

Mix well. Just before eating, dress with:
2 Tablespoons light salad dressing (red wine vinaigrette, light Italian, or light balsamic)

- ✓ Yield: 1-1/2 cup
- ✓ Calories: 185
- ✓ Protein: 12.9 grams
- ✓ Carbohydrate: 6.4 grams
- ✓ Fat: 13.2 grams

Chicken and Apple Slaw

Chicken salad can be made a number of different ways. This recipe adds some appealing crunchy texture with the cabbage, apple, and seeds. The protein will leave you feeling satisfied and energized. To save time and frustration, buy the cabbage prewashed and precut in a bag (sometimes it will be packaged as "stir-fry mix"). It keeps much longer than bagged lettuce greens.

- 2 ounces shredded chicken breast
- 3/4 cup shredded green and red cabbage
- 1/2 apple, peeled and cubed
- 1 Tablespoon slivered almonds, sunflower seeds, or pumpkin seeds

Mix well. Just before eating, dress with:
1 Tablespoon light ranch, light caesar, or light slaw dressing

- ✓ Yield: 1 cup
- ✓ Calories: 240
- ✓ Protein: 20 grams
- ✓ Carbohydrate: 19.5 grams
- ✓ Fat: 9.7 grams

Dinner

My dinners are more like suppers. I like to keep things simple by fixing a main dish consisting of meat and vegetables. For soups, I serve a low-fat spread and crackers on the side. The cleanup is amazingly easy when you only use one or two pans and fresh, simple ingredients.

Shrimp and Asparagus Stir-Fry

I love shrimp! It has huge amounts of protein and almost no fat. If your grocery store is in a medium size or large city, the fish counter will sell fresh or thawed, previously-frozen shrimp in the display case. Don't be shy about asking how long ago it was brought in, or its sell-by date. If the store doesn't sell a lot of seafood, opt for bags of precooked frozen shrimp, which aren't as good as fresh but are uniform quality. Buy your shrimp peeled and deveined because life is too short to spend processing shrimp! This recipe pits the gorgeous pink color of the shrimp against bright green asparagus and tastes as good as it looks.

- 10 to 14 asparagus spears with tough part of the stalk trimmed off
- 1 pound medium size peeled and deveined shrimp, raw or precooked
- 1 teaspoon garlic (freshly pressed or paste)
- 1 Tablespoon lemon juice
- Cooking spray
- Optional: 1 Tablespoon fresh or dried parsley

Steam the asparagus until tender. Rinse the shrimp and pat dry between paper towels. Spray a large nonstick frying pan with cooking spray. Start with the shrimp if you purchased it raw and stir-fry over medium-high heat until it's pink all the way through. Turn heat up to high and add the asparagus, lemon juice, and garlic (and shrimp if precooked). Sear all ingredients, tossing constantly with a spatula, until hot and slightly browned on their surfaces. Remove from heat, toss in fresh parsley, and serve immediately.

- ✓ Yield: 3/4 cup
- ✓ Calories: 200
- ✓ Protein: 24 grams
- ✓ Carbohydrate: 5 grams
- ✓ Fat: 7 grams

Baked Salmon with Pesto

Salmon is easy to find in the fish display case of your grocery store, and the price per pound is reasonable if you opt for farm-raised. Be sure to ask about the sell-by date! Don't settle for frozen unless nothing else is available. Salmon is a nutritionally dense food, so eat it slowly until you learn how your body handles it. Even if you're dining alone, go ahead and purchase a 12-ounce filet, bake the whole thing, and divide it into four portions to eat for lunch and dinner.

- 3 ounces of fresh farm-raised salmon, rinsed and patted dry between paper towels
- 1 Tablespoon reduced-fat pesto sauce (look in the cooler in the Italian foods aisle of your grocery store)
- Cooking spray

Preheat oven to 325. Spray a square of nonstick foil with cooking spray, place it on a cookie sheet, and turn up the edges to make a tray. Place the filet on the foil with the skin facing down. Spread 1 Tablespoon per 3 ounces of fish over the salmon. Bake for 30 minutes, or until the thickest part of the filet is light pink all the way through. Separate the fish from its skin with a metal spatula. Serve with a steamed vegetable or green salad with light dressing.

- ✓ Yield: 1-1/4 cup
- ✓ Calories: 228
- ✓ Protein: 20.4 grams
- ✓ Carbohydrate: 1.8grams
- ✓ Fat: 14.4 grams

Italian Sole

Any mild white fish can be livened up with an Italian pasta sauce. Choose sole, tilapia, cod, or farm raised catfish. The variety isn't as important as the freshness, so check the sell-by date on the package. For the marinara sauce, check the jar for added sugar before you buy it, because some brands like to sneak the sweet stuff in. You can also look for fresh marinara in the cooler in the Italian foods aisle.

- Marinara sauce, 1/3 cup per 3 ounces of fish
- 3 ounces mild white fish, rinsed and patted dry between paper towels
- 1 teaspoon lemon juice
- 1 Tablespoon sliced black olives
- 1/2 cup sliced fresh mushrooms
- 1 teaspoon garlic (freshly pressed or paste)
- Cooking spray

Spray a large nonstick frying pan with cooking spray. Add the mushrooms and the fish and toss occasionally until cooked all the way through, allowing the fish to break up into flakes. Add the marinara, lemon juice, olives, and garlic, mix well, and heat thoroughly.

- ✓ Yield: 1 cup
- ✓ Calories: 174
- ✓ Protein: 22 grams
- ✓ Carbohydrate: 8 grams
- ✓ Fat: 5 grams

Baked Orange Sole

Citrus fruit is wonderful for driving away the faint fishy taste you sometimes get with white fish. If you're careful to only buy recently stocked fish that hasn't been frozen, you'll like the results of this simple, versatile fish recipe that can be used for just about any mild white fish. You'll love the high protein and the incredibly low fat content.

- 3 ounces of sole or other white fish, rinsed and patted dry between paper towels
- 1 orange or grapefruit, cut into thin slices
- Cooking spray

Preheat oven to 325. Spray a square of nonstick foil with cooking spray, place it on a cookie sheet, and turn up the edges to make a tray. Lay the fish on the foil and cover with the citrus slices. Bake for 15-20 minutes, or until the fish is baked all the way through and flakes easily. Peel away and discard the fruit and use a metal spatula to carefully separate the fish from the foil. Serve with sliced avocados or steamed fresh or frozen peas.

- ✓ Yield: 1 cup
- ✓ Calories: 100
- ✓ Protein: 20.5 grams
- ✓ Carbohydrate: 0 grams
- ✓ Fat: 1.3 grams

ROSEMARY DOLLOFF

Pan-Fried Scallops and Summer Squash

Scallops are incredibly tasty for being so inexpensive, and I like their neat, little round shape, like small cakes. Sea scallops are actually firm white fish cut into a round shape and sold frozen. They're less expensive than real scallops and are the easiest to find at the grocery store. If you buy fresh scallops, pay especially close attention to the sell-by date, because shoppers who don't know how good they are tend to overlook them and cause stock to back up. Don't skip the lemon juice when you prepare this recipe.

- 4 fresh scallops or sea scallops (about 3 ounces per serving)
- 1/2 cup summer squash, cubed
- 6 cherry tomatoes, sliced in half
- 1 teaspoon olive oil
- 1 teaspoon garlic (freshly pressed or paste)
- 1 Tablespoon lemon juice
- 2 Tablespoons dry white wine (can be nonalcoholic)

In a large nonstick frying pan, heat the olive oil and garlic on medium. Turn heat to medium-high and add the zucchini and scallops, tossing occasionally with a spatula until cooked all the way through. Add the cherry tomatoes, lemon juice, and wine and mix well. Cover and steam for five minutes until the tomatoes start to soften. Serve with ripe olives or capers on the side.

- ✓ Yield: 1-1/2 cup
- ✓ Calories: 241
- ✓ Protein: 20.6 grams
- ✓ Carbohydrate: 9.4 grams
- ✓ Fat: 6 grams

Pan-Roasted Chicken

Boneless, skinless chicken breasts are the heart of your weight-loss strategy after surgery. They're so convenient, and they can be sectioned into the right size portion for your eating plan. They also pack a powerful protein punch, with very few calories or grams of fat. Wait for them to go on sale, then buy a bundle of them and toss them in the freezer. If you eat by yourself, fix four 4-ounce filets at a time for lunches or an easy dinner after work.(A 4-ounce uncooked filet will reduce to 3 ounces after cooking.)

- Boneless, skinless chicken breast, 4 uncooked ounces per serving
- 1 teaspoon olive oil
- 1 teaspoon garlic (freshly pressed or paste)
- 2 Tablespoons dry white wine (can be nonalcoholic)
- 2 Tablespoons drained capers

In a large nonstick frying pan, heat the olive oil and garlic on medium. Turn heat to medium-high and add the chicken breasts, tossing occasionally with a spatula until browned. Add the wine and capers, cover, and reduce heat to low. Steam for about 15 minutes, or until chicken is no longer pink in the center.

- ✓ Yield: 1-1/2 cup
- ✓ Calories: 198
- ✓ Protein: 27 grams
- ✓ Carbohydrate: 1.2 grams
- ✓ Fat: 7.7 grams

Chicken and Pesto

This recipe features intense flavors to make boneless, skinless chicken breasts a fresh experience with a Mediterranean flair. The sun-dried tomatoes can be chewy, so experiment to make sure they agree with you after your surgery. If you've kept your carbohydrates low all day so far, you can spoon this delectable mixture over a small helping of angel hair pasta or fettucine, boiled until tender.

- Boneless, skinless chicken breast, 4 uncooked ounces per serving
- 1 Tablespoon reduced-fat pesto sauce (look in the cooler in the Italian foods aisle of your grocery store)
- 4 large sun-dried tomatoes, drained and chopped
- 2 Tablespoons dry white wine (can be nonalcoholic)
- Cooking spray

Spray a large nonstick frying pan with cooking spray. Over medium-high heat, brown the chicken breasts on both sides. Add the wine, pesto sauce, and tomatoes and toss. Reduce heat to low and cover. Steam for about 15 minutes, or until chicken is no longer pink in the center.

- ✓ Yield: 1 cup
- ✓ Calories: 227
- ✓ Protein: 29.4 grams
- ✓ Carbohydrate: 6.7 grams
- ✓ Fat: 7.2 grams

Grilled Chicken Italian Style

Outdoor grilling is wildly popular for some excellent reasons. Hands down, it's the best way to preserve the flavor of meat while getting rid of the excess fat by letting it sizzle away. It's also an reason to get out on the deck and enjoy the great outdoors. Like all meats, chicken has to be watched carefully and turned frequently to avoid drying it out. Use a pair of metal tongs to flip the chicken pieces frequently. The signature crisscross pattern on the meat is created by repositioning them at a 90 degree angle on the grill grate after starting them.

- Boneless, skinless chicken breast, 4 uncooked ounces per serving
- 3 rings sliced bell pepper, any color
- Sweet white onion, one slice
- 2 Tablespoons grated parmesan or romano cheese
- 1 teaspoon dried oregano
- Cooking spray

Start the grill on medium high. Spray the chicken breast on both sides with cooking spray and sprinkle with oregano. Grill for 4-8 minutes on each side, depending on thickness, until chicken is no longer pink in the middle. Spray a small frying pan with cooking spray. Cook the pepper and onion over medium high heat until tender. Dress the chicken piece with the vegetables and top with the grated cheese.

- ✓ Yield: 1 cup
- ✓ Calories: 192
- ✓ Protein: 30.7 grams
- ✓ Carbohydrate: 2 grams
- ✓ Fat: 6 grams

Chicken Lettuce Wraps

These wraps are low fat, low carb, and low calorie, and they make for an attractive presentation. For convenience, you can buy precut large lettuce leaves for wrapping in many grocery stores, or you can use iceberg, which holds its shape and texture even when filled with warm ingredients. Preshredded carrots are available in the bagged salad section of most stores and further cut down on preparation time. These wraps need to be eaten right away after stuffing so the lettuce doesn't wilt.

Boneless, skinless chicken breast, diced into 1/2 inch pieces, 4 uncooked ounces per serving
- 1 Tablespoon chopped green onion tops
- 1 6 inch stalk of celery, chopped
- 1/4 cup shredded carrot
- 1 teaspoon low sodium soy sauce
- Cooking spray
- 1 large lettuce leaf

Spray a large nonstick frying pan with cooking spray. Over medium-high heat, toss the diced chicken pieces until browned and cooked all the way through. Stir in the onion, carrots, and celery and toss until warm. Mix in the soy sauce. Spoon into the lettuce leaf, fold into a roll, and serve immediately.

- ✓ Yield: 1 cup
- ✓ Calories: 157
- ✓ Protein: 27.8 grams
- ✓ Carbohydrate: 3 grams
- ✓ Fat: 3.2 grams

Chicken Tortellini Salad

Tortellini is a pocket of pasta stuffed with cheese, vegetables, chicken, or seafood. They tend to be higher in calories than other pasta, so a little goes a long way, but they're also very satisfying, especially when paired with poultry. The secret of cooking tortellini is to watch it carefully and drain it when it's tender but not so tender that it cracks and loses its filling. This tasty salad is marinated, so it can be made in advance and stored in the refrigerator until ready to eat or pack in a leakproof container for lunch at work.

- 1/3 cup cooked cheese tortellini
- Boneless, skinless chicken breast, diced into 1 inch pieces, 4 uncooked ounces per serving
- 1 Tablespoon chopped red onion
- 1 Tablespoon sliced black olives
- 1 Tablespoon light balsamic salad dressing

Boil the tortellini until tender, drain, and cool. Spray a large nonstick frying pan with cooking spray. Over medium-high heat, toss the diced chicken pieces until browned and cooked all the way through, and allow to cool. In a medium size bowl, mix the tortellini, chicken, onion, olives, and salad dressing thoroughly. Chill in the refrigerator for an hour before eating.

- ✓ Yield: 1 cup
- ✓ Calories: 278
- ✓ Protein: 31.6 grams
- ✓ Carbohydrate: 16 grams
- ✓ Fat: 8.8 grams

Turkey Chili

This chili is low in fat and can go from mild to wild by adjusting the amount of chili powder and jalapeno pepper. Jalapenos give chili that authentic Mexican taste and are fairly mild as long as you don't use too much. Cut them up wearing rubber kitchen gloves and use a sharp knife to take out the seeds and ribs. Don't wipe your face or eyes until you've washed the knife, removed the gloves, and washed your hands.

- 1 pound uncooked ground turkey breast
- 4 Tablespoons chopped onion
- 4 Tablespoons chopped green bell pepper
- 1/2 to 1 fresh jalapeno pepper, minced very fine
- 1 cup low sodium, fat free chicken broth
- 1 16-ounce can crushed tomatoes, not drained
- 1/2 to 2 teaspoons chili powder
- Cooking spray

Spray a large nonstick frying pan with cooking spray. Over medium-high heat, cook the ground turkey until nearly done while separating into small pieces using the edge of a spatula. Add the onion, bell pepper, and jalapeno and toss until softened.

In a soup pot, combine the chicken broth, tomatoes, and chili powder. Add the turkey and vegetables. Add water to cover the solid ingredients. Cover and bring to a boil, then reduce heat and simmer gently for 1 hour before serving.

- ✓ Yield: Four 1 cup servings
- ✓ Calories: 171
- ✓ Protein: 30 grams
- ✓ Carbohydrate: 10.5 grams
- ✓ Fat: 1 grams

Stir-Fried Turkey and Broccoli

This Asian-style dish goes together in a flash and features high protein with very low fat. You can find whole turkey breast in the frozen poultry section of your grocery store. It's sold uncooked or precooked, and either one will work for this recipe, but be sure to note which one you've purchased. The secret of a good stir-fry is to use high heat to seal in the moisture in the ingredients instead of cooking it out. The broccoli is steamed ahead of time to make sure it will be tender.

- Boneless turkey breast, diced into 1/2 inch pieces, 4 uncooked ounces per serving
- 1/2 cup chopped broccoli florets
- 1 Tablespoon chopped sweet onion
- 1 teaspoon low-sodium soy sauce
- 1 Tablespoon low-sodium teriyaki sauce
- Cooking spray

Steam the broccoli lightly for 8 to 10 minutes and drain thoroughly. Set aside. Spray a large nonstick frying pan with cooking spray. Brown the turkey and onion over medium-high heat until cooked all the way through. Turn heat up to high. Add the broccoli, soy sauce, and teriyaki sauce and toss with a spatula until ingredients begin to form a crust on their surfaces. Serve with additional soy sauce.

- ✓ Yield: 1 cup
- ✓ Calories: 184
- ✓ Protein: 32.5 grams
- ✓ Carbohydrate: 11 grams
- ✓ Fat: 1.2 grams

Ham and Winter Squash Soup

This recipe is hearty and filling on cold winter nights. The squash takes time to bake, but the recipe itself is super easy. Serve it with low-fat cream cheese on rice crackers and you have a full meal.

- 1 acorn or 1/2 butternut squash
- 1/2 sweet onion, chopped
- 1 cup skim milk
- 2 cups fat-free, low-sodium chicken broth
- Cooking spray
- 2 cups diced cooked ham
- Salt and pepper to taste

Preheat oven to 350. Bake the squash whole on a cookie sheet lined with parchment paper or foil until it starts to soften, about 1 hour. Slice the squash lengthwise, spray the paper or foil with cooking spray, and place the two halves cut side down. Bake 30 minutes more, or until squash is soft and tender throughout. Allow squash to cool. Scoop out the seeds and discard. Scoop out the squash into a soup pot. Whisk in the milk and broth until mixed thoroughly. Add the onion, ham, and spices, and simmer 30 minutes over low heat until onions are tender.

- ✓ Yield: Four 1-cup servings
- ✓ Calories: 163
- ✓ Protein: 13 grams
- ✓ Carbohydrate: 11.9 grams
- ✓ Fat: 4.3 grams

Grilled Pork Chop with Chutney Sauce

Pork chops and chutney sauce were made for each other. The complex flavors of the fruits, vinegar, and spices of the chutney complement the sweet flavor of good pork. Thicker chops tend to be better cuts of meat, so if they run over your allowed weight, bag half of the chop and save it for lunch or dinner the next day. This recipe can be adapted to pan-frying by using a nonstick pan and cooking spray if the weather doesn't allow you to use the grill.

- Boneless or bone-in pork chop, 4 uncooked ounces per serving
- 2 Tablespoons light balsamic salad dressing for marinade
- 1/4 teaspoon garlic powder
- 2 Tablespoons mango chutney

Pour the balsamic salad dressing in a shallow square dish just large enough to hold the pork chop. Marinate for 20 minutes on one side; turn, and marinate the other side. Set aside the marinade. Heat the grill to medium-high. Sprinkle the chop with the garlic powder on each side. Grill for 3 to 7 minutes per side, depending on the thickness of the chop. Grill until the meat has lost its pink color in the middle, but do not allow it to dry out. Place grilled chop on a plate and spoon chutney over the top. Serve with a light dinner salad dressed with lemon juice.

- ✓ Yield: 1 cup
- ✓ Calories: 254
- ✓ Protein: 24.4 grams
- ✓ Carbohydrate: 11 grams
- ✓ Fat: 11.6 grams

Pork Kebabs

Kebabs are colorful, convenient, and tasty. It's worthwhile to invest in metal skewers so you don't have to worry about the wooden ones catching fire while cooking. If you only have the wooden ones, soak them in water for 24 hours before creating the kebabs and you shouldn't have any problems with combustion. The eating style for kebabs is a matter of personal preference. Most people use a fork to gently coax the grilled pieces off the skewer onto the plate, but they can also be treated as finger food, especially at outdoor picnics.

- Pork tenderloin, 4 uncooked ounces per serving
- 4 button mushrooms
- 4 onion pieces
- 2 bell pepper pieces, any color
- 2 cherry tomatoes
- 1 tablespoon light balsamic vinegar salad dressing

Trim the fat from the pork loin and cut into 1-inch cubes. Toss in a small bowl with the salad dressing until coated. Wash the mushrooms and pat dry. Cut the onion into 1-inch pieces by separating each layer. Cut the bell pepper into 1-inch pieces. Wash and dry the cherry tomatoes. Heat the grill to medium-high. Spear the kebab ingredients onto skewers, alternating each ingredient to create a mix. Lay the skewers across the grill and rotate frequently until the pork is cooked all the way through.

- ✓ Yield: 1 cup
- ✓ Calories: 220
- ✓ Protein: 25.8 grams
- ✓ Carbohydrate: 5 grams
- ✓ Fat: 10.4 grams

Pan-Fried Sirloin with Mushroom Gravy

This classic steak recipe makes the most of the combination of sirloin and mushrooms. Unground beef can be tricky to digest after surgery, so be sure to chew the steak thoroughly and test your reaction to it by eating only a few bites at a time. If you tolerate it well, go ahead and enjoy the high protein content of beef, as long as you trim off the excess fat.

- Choice sirloin steak, 4 ounces per serving
- 1/2 cup sliced mushrooms
- 1 Tablespoon chopped sweet onion
- 1 teaspoon olive oil
- 2/3 cup low-sodium, fat-free beef broth
- 1 teaspoon arrowroot powder or 1 tablespoon white flour
- 1/2 teaspoon dried thyme
- 1/4 teaspoon black pepper
- Cooking spray

Trim all fat from the steak. Spray a large nonstick frying pan with cooking spray. Over medium-high heat, brown the steak on both sides. Reduce heat and continue to cook until done to taste. Remove the meat from the pan and cover it to keep it warm. Heat the olive oil in the pan, add the onions and mushrooms, and toss until tender. Add the arrowroot or flour and stir until all ingredients are coated. Gradually stir in the beef broth. Add the pepper and thyme and simmer until thickened. Return the beef to the pan and cook until hot enough to serve.

- ✓ Yield: 1 cup
- ✓ Calories: 229
- ✓ Protein: 29.4 grams
- ✓ Carbohydrate: 12.3 grams
- ✓ Fat: 6.4 grams

Meatloaf

Your mother's meatloaf can make the transition to post-weight loss surgery if you use a very lean cut of ground beef, like sirloin, and rely on egg substitute as a binder. One more thing: hold the ketchup. Read the label – you'll be amazed at how much sugar sneaks into that innocent bottle of ketchup sitting in your fridge. If you're traditional and love ketchup on your meatloaf, choose a sugar-free substitute, often sold in the diabetic foods section of larger supermarkets.

- 1 pound ground beef sirloin
- 4 Tablespoons chopped white onion
- 1/2 cup egg substitute
- 1 teaspoon garlic powder
- 1 teaspoon dried thyme
- 1/2 teaspoon black pepper
- 1 Tablespoon Worcestershire sauce
- Cooking spray

Preheat oven to 350. Mix the ground beef and egg substitute thoroughly in a large mixing bowl. Add the onion, spices, and Worcestershire sauce, and mix until well distributed Spray a glass or metal loaf pan with cooking spray. Pour the meatloaf mixture into the pan and distribute evenly. Bake 45 to 60 minutes, until meatloaf starts to shrink away from the edges of the pan. Serve with sugar-free ketchup if desired.

- ✓ Yield: four 1-cup servings
- ✓ Calories: 212
- ✓ Protein: 32.8 grams
- ✓ Carbohydrate: 1.5 grams
- ✓ Fat: 7.4 grams

Beef Stew

This stew is a winter favorite because it's so warming and comforting. Although the stew meat requires some simmering time to become tender, it's not difficult to make, and it can sit on the stove on autopilot while you do other things. If you prefer a crock pot or slow cooker, use the low setting and let it simmer for 8 hours while you're at work so you can come home to a tasty hot meal already prepared for you.

- 8 ounces of beef stew meat, cubed
- 1/2 white sweet onion, chopped
- 4 medium size carrots, peeled and chopped into 1/2 inch rounds
- 1 medium size white or red potato, peeled and cut into 3/4 inch cubes
- 2 cups low-sodium, fat-free beef broth
- Salt and pepper to taste
- Cooking spray

Trim away any excess fat from the stew meat. Spray a large nonstick frying pan with cooking spray. Over medium-high heat, sear the stew meat on all sides and set aside. Pour the beef broth into a soup pot. Add the stew meat with juice from the pan, salt and pepper. Bring to a boil. Reduce heat and simmer gently for 90 minutes until beef starts to become tender. Increase heat to medium high and add the onion, carrots, and potato. Bring back to a boil, then reduce heat again and simmer for 20 minutes until vegetables are tender.

- ✓ Yield: two 1-cup servings
- ✓ Calories: 240
- ✓ Protein: 28.7 grams
- ✓ Carbohydrate: 20.2 grams
- ✓ Fat: 4.6 grams

Lamb Burgers with Feta Cheese

Ground lamb is a wonderful change from ground beef. It's rich and flavorful and accepts seasonings with ease. The frozen spinach and feta cheese add to the Greek character of this dish. You can serve the burgers plain and eat them with a knife and fork, or insert them in half a pita bread pocket to keep them from getting messy while you eat them with your hands. These work equally well on the grill, or in a nonstick frying pan coated with cooking spray.

- 1 pound ground lamb
- 1/2 cup egg substitute
- 1/2 cup feta cheese
- 1 8 ounce package frozen spinach

Mix the ground lamb, egg substitute, and feta cheese thoroughly in a large mixing bowl. Drain the spinach thoroughly in a colander and press all of the water out with your fingers. Blot the spinach dry between two paper towels. Chop it fine and add it to the ground lamb mixture. Form the mixture into burger patties 4 inches in diameter. Grill or pan-fry until done to taste, from medium rare to medium.

- ✓ Yield: four 1-cup servings
- ✓ Calories: 266
- ✓ Protein: 32.8 grams
- ✓ Carbohydrate: 2.8 grams
- ✓ Fat: 13.2 grams

Stuffed Portobello Mushrooms

Those huge portobello mushrooms make a wonderful meal when you want a dish with very little meat added. Roasted in the oven, they have the texture and flavor of steak, but without the fat and calories. This recipe features a stuffing that you can vary to suit your moods or to use up leftover vegetables from the fridge. In warm weather it can be grilled outdoors for a special summer treat.

- 1 extra large portobello mushroom per serving (5 inches diameter)
- 1 slice hard salami, chopped
- 4 large sun-dried tomatoes, drained and chopped
- 1/4 cup low-fat shredded mozzarella cheese
- Light balsamic salad dressing

Preheat oven to 375. Brush mushroom with salad dressing on both sides and place smooth side down in a small glass baking dish. Mix salami and tomatoes thoroughly and spoon into the mushroom cavity. Cover with foil and bake for 15-20 minutes until mushroom is tender in the center. Top with cheese, uncover, and serve as soon as cheese melts with a side salad.

- ✓ Yield: 1 cup
- ✓ Calories: 192
- ✓ Protein: 15.7 grams
- ✓ Carbohydrate: 17.9 grams
- ✓ Fat: 8.9 grams

ROSEMARY DOLLOFF

Green Beans with Bacon

Bacon makes a great, protein-rich addition to a light, vegetable-based dinner. Nitrate and nitrite free brands are now available in most grocery stores, and baking it in the oven minimizes the fat content and the mess to clean up afterward. You can bake several slices at once and bag them in individual servings to add later to salads, or to warm up in the microwave for lunch. Be sure to cover bacon if you microwave it!

Baked Bacon:

Preheat oven to 360
2 strips bacon
Line a cookie sheet or baking dish with foil, crushed slightly to allow air to circulate
Bake for 20-30 minutes until bacon is crisp and snip into bite size pieces with kitchen shears

Main dish:

- 1 cup fresh or frozen green beans
- 1 Tablespoon chopped sweet onion
- 1 Tablespoon chopped walnuts, almonds, or pecans
- 1 Tablespoon rice vinegar or 2 teaspoons white wine or balsamic vinegar
- Cooking spray

Steam green beans until tender and drain thoroughly. Spray a medium size skillet with cooking spray. Toss green beans, onions, and nuts until slightly browned. Add the bacon and the vinegar, toss thoroughly, and serve.

- ✓ Yield: 1 cup
- ✓ Calories: 204
- ✓ Protein: 9.2 grams
- ✓ Carbohydrate: 12.5 grams
- ✓ Fat: 15 grams

Baked Tofu

Tofu doesn't get enough credit as a tasty food, probably because it's so bland when prepared without seasonings. Marinating it transforms its character into a flavor bomb, and coated with tasty panko bread crumbs, it's every bit as good as the chicken nuggets I used to eat to excess, but without the fat, preservatives, and calories. Purchasing extra firm tofu and pressing out every last bit of water is crucial to getting a good result with this recipe.

- 1 8-ounce package extra firm tofu
- 1 teaspoon canola or grapeseed oil

- 1 teaspoon low-sodium soy sauce
- 1 Tablespoon low-sodium teriyaki sauce
- 1/2 cup panko bread crumbs
- Cooking spray

Press the water out of the tofu block by placing it between two paper towels and balancing a heavy frying pan on top of it for five minutes. Cut the tofu into slices 1/4 inch thick. Preheat the oven to 350. Prepare the marinade by shaking the oil, soy sauce, and teriyaki sauce in a jar. Pour it into a flat, shallow pan or baking dish and distribute the tofu slices across the bottom. Soak them for 10 minutes, flip them, and soak the other side for 5 minutes. Spray a cookie sheet with cooking spray. Pour the panko bread crumbs on a plate. Dip each tofu slice in the crumbs, flip, and dip again to coat it on both sides. Arrange the tofu slices on the cookie sheet and bake for 10 minutes, then flip and bake on the other side until the panko crumbs are crispy golden brown.

- Yield: two 1-cup servings
- Calories: 210
- Protein: 14.3 grams
- Carbohydrate: 20.1 grams
- Fat: 9 grams

Snacks

My meal plan called for two snacks per day, but yours might allow three. In any case, regular eating is important to keep hunger at bay and to regulate your blood sugar. The challenge is not to let snacking get out of control and turn into a fourth and fifth meal. You don't want to succeed with surgery and your three meals per day, only to sabotage yourself which snacks that are too big. I'm a big fan of prepackaged snack foods because they're portion-controlled, so I'm not tempted to overindulge. They're also super convenient so I don't have to drop what I'm doing while I eat on the fly.

ROSEMARY DOLLOFF

Protein Powder Shake

The secret of a tasty protein powder drink is a mixing bottle with a tightly sealed lid and a mixer ball. These balls look like little round wire cages, and when you shake them, they break up those nasty of lumps of protein powder that tend to linger at the bottom of the cup. A 20 ounce size is plenty big enough, and you shouldn't have to pay more than $10 for one, so go ahead and get two so you'll always have a clean one on hand.

I have many favorite brands and flavors of protein shake mixes, and I like to give myself as much variety as possible so I don't get tired of them. I have just a few requirements when I go shopping. Shakes should be fewer than 5 grams of sugar per serving, and no soy protein added – I don't digest it well, and I prefer whey protein for its nutritional value. Oh, and one more requirement: it has to be on sale. These things are expensive, so watch for a special deal and go stock up. In the summer, I toss in a couple of ice cubes, or blend the cubes with the drink if I'm near a blender. In cold months, I mix the a coffee, chocolate, or vanilla flavor with hot water, coffee or tea for a hot comfort beverage.

Some of the brands I like include:
- Now Foods
- Met-RX
- Believe
- Inspire
- Designer Whey

Brands vary in nutritional makeup, so I've selected one scoop of Designer Whey to use as an example.
- ✓ Yield: 1 cup
- ✓ Calories: 100
- ✓ Protein: 18 grams
- ✓ Carbohydrate: 3 grams
- ✓ Fat: 2 grams

ROSEMARY DOLLOFF

Protein Bars

Before my surgery, I was constantly snacking on "energy bars," unaware that the leading brands are major sugar bombs, packing a whopping 20 grams per bar, or higher. I'm pretty sure they contributed heavily to my weight gain. When I decided to have surgery, I started reading food labels and crossed most of those brands off my list. I still love the convenience of protein bars, so I've switched to the ones containing artificial sweetener and as much protein content as I can get. My requirements are a bit different from protein shakes. I want fewer than 5 grams of sugar per serving, and whey protein should be high on the list of ingredients and soy protein should be low. Of course they should be on sale. There's a catch with protein bars: they're too big for one serving! To avoid sabotaging your meal plan, cut one in half right after you eat breakfast and seal each half in a plastic bag. Pack them in separate spots in your lunch kit, or put one half away in the cupboard if you're home, so you aren't tempted to double dip.

Here's a brief list of some of my favorite brands:
- Met-RX
- Atkins Advantage
- Quest
- Power Crunch

Here's a sample nutritional breakdown for half of an Atkins Advantage Strawberry Almond bar.
- ✓ Yield: 1/2 bar
- ✓ Calories: 100
- ✓ Protein: 7.5 grams
- ✓ Carbohydrate: 10 grams
- ✓ Fat: 4.5 grams

ROSEMARY DOLLOFF

Ready-to-Drink Protein Shakes

People love convenience, and I'm right there with them. I was surprised by the number of ready-to-drink shakes on the market, and a fair number of them are low in sugar. Just watch those labels like a hawk – some of the well known brands are loaded with the sweet stuff. They're non-perishable, so your best bet is to order them online if you can't find them where you shop.

My favorite brands include:
- Met-RX
- Atkins Advantage
- Isopure
- 20/20 Lifestyles
- Oh Yeah!

Here's a sample nutritional breakdown for an Atkins Advantage Protein Shake.
- Yield: 1 cup
- Calories: 160
- Protein: 15 grams
- Carbohydrate: 5 grams
- Fat: 10 grams

Fat-Free Low-Sugar Yogurt

Yogurt was another wake-up call for me when I started reading food labels. Flavored yogurt contains an average of 20 grams of sugar and was yet another diet buster for me before I had surgery. Yogurt naturally contains some sugar from the milk it's made with, so any added sweetener needs to be sugar free. You can also make your own low-sugar yogurt by buying Dannon Plain Fat-Free and adding your favorite artificial sweetener and a sugar-free flavoring.

I did some detective work and came up with a list of low-sugar, low-fat yogurt brands. Not all of them will be available in your area, but Dannon should be sold just about anywhere.

- Dannon Light 'n Fit
- Kroger Lite
- Kroger CarbMaster
- Archer Farms
- Blue Bunny

Here's a sample nutritional profile for Dannon Light 'n Fit cherry flavor with 11 grams of sugar.

- ✓ Yield: 6 ounce cup
- ✓ Calories: 80
- ✓ Protein: 5 grams

- ✓ Carbohydrate: 16 grams
- ✓ Fat: 0 grams

Cheese Stick and Fruit

When I get tired of ready-to eat snacks and want something more natural, a low-fat cheese stick and a small serving of fruit are a nice change of pace. Cheese sticks are usually made of mozzarella cheese, which is low in fat and comes in its own convenient wrapper. Your fruit serving should total 1/2 cup.

Serving sizes for particular fruits are given below.
- Half a large apple
- Half a pear
- Half a large peach
- 2 small apricots

- 1 plum or nectarine
- 4 large or 6 medium size strawberries
- 10 raspberries
- 1 kiwi fruit
- 1/2 large orange or grapefruit, or 1 tangerine

✓ Yield: one 0.7 ounce cheese stick and 1/2 cup of fruit
✓ Calories: 91
✓ Protein: 5.6 grams
✓ Carbohydrate: 7.7 grams
✓ Fat: 4.6 grams

Made in the USA
Middletown, DE
13 September 2016